Plan YOUR Perfect Wedding in 90 Days!

By J. H. Dies

A Newbiz Playbook Publication

FIRST EDITION

ISBN-13: 978-1542472845

For free downloadable tools emailed directly to you please email proof of purchase of this book to products@newbizplaybook.com use the password 90 Days in the re: of the email

For my family, the answer to my why

Understanding The Task in Front of You

You have been thinking about this day for much of your life. The size of the task in front of you depends to some degree on the size of your event.

If you event will be at home, or a venue owned or controlled by a friend or family member. It will be easier.

If your event will be supplied by food you, and friends or family provide, it will (in some ways) be easier.

Each professional and/or venue you hire adds to the complexity of this undertaking. Be sure to check bonus vendor tools to help you coordinate

We did not assume that your budget allows for any professionals, so we provided tools to help you be your own!

Not to worry, this book is designed to help you get it all done, from the simplest of weddings, to the most elaborate shindig imaginable in 90 days!

So a word or two about how to use this book, and then we will get after it right now. Remember to use the tools.

This book is written as a descending time line starting at that 90 day mark. If you are inside of 90 days, get the work done until you are caught up with the timeline. Certain aspects of this plan will take time, so don't take the chronology recommendations likely.

We don't want you to get jammed!

Chapter 1 - 90 Days Out

This part of the process may feel a bit frenetic. For larger, more elaborate events, we are a bit behind. If your event will be smaller with no venue or few hired professionals you are right on time. To make sure we don't forget important tasks, be sure to email us for the electronic checklist at products@newbizplaybook.com.

Regardless of the complexity of your event, or the time you have, this is still the order that should be followed in planning your event.

Immediately after the engagement 90 days:

_____ Choose a wedding date and time.

_____ Send engagement announcement to newspapers.

_____ Hire photographer – (See the interview attachment at the end of this chapter) – if you are your own photographer, or getting help see our tool for that

_____ Book engagement photo session with enough time to submit photos to local newspapers.

_____ Discuss a budget with your fiancé and whoever may be assisting in paying for the wedding, and determine who/which family will pay for various aspects of the wedding. Key decisions about number of guests, and scope should be discussed.

_____ Consider making lists of who must be invited, who should be invited, and who it would be nice to invite to help narrow the guest list.

_____ First pass at wedding party including ring and flower bearers

_____ Evaluate venues, and check availability. - THIS IS A HUGE PRIORITY BECAUSE AVAILABILITY WILL BE LIMITED – see our venue evaluation tool at the end of this chapter.

_____ If you and or your family/friends are going to be the venue, and the reception will be held at a home, or on the land of friends or family, you can address inside 60 days – see our tools for all things reception planning after Chapter 2.

_____ Make arrangements for the music at the wedding and reception. – See DJ planning tool at the end of this chapter

_____ Make all transportation arrangements to and from the wedding.

_____ Make arrangements for passports if needed

_____ Create a binder to organize your thoughts, photos, worksheets, etc.

_____ Make initial contact with vendors and obtain references.

_____ Meet with clergy member; schedule pre-marital counseling if that is part of your belief system or something you will need.

_____ make initial catering decisions and sign contract – see catering interview checklist at the end of this chapter,

_____ If you or your family/friends will handle food and/or alcohol, you will need to price your menu – use our food and beverage planning tool at the end of this chapter. It provides amounts for almost any menu, and you can use those to shop and determine your food and beverage costs.

_____ Consider color palettes and dress for parties at wedding.

_____ Register at local bridal registries.

_____ Finalize the attendants (bridesmaids and groomsmen). Choose and order bridesmaids dresses.

_____ Select one usher for every 50 guests.

_____ Finalize the guest list.

_____ Complete Guest list management tool and VIP contact tool– attached after this chapter to help with invitations, date cards, and rsvp information

_____ Send out Save the Date cards.

_____ Reserve a block of hotel rooms for out-of-town guests.

_____ Choose wedding rings.

_____ Select and order wedding gown, leaving ample time for delivery and alterations.

_____ Look for alteration specialist (if some- one other than bridal shop).

_____ Purchase invitations.

_____ Schedule wedding cake design appointment if other than caterer

_____ Plan beauty preparations by checking with your salon for how far in advance they book wedding parties.

_____ Finalize all honeymoon plans. If traveling outside the country, check on visas, passports and inoculations.

_____ Sign up for dance lessons. Talk to instructor about choreographing a special dance routine to "wow" guests.

_____ Book venue and all professionals securing dates by putting down deposit if applicable

_____ Confirm menu details with the caterer.

_____ Order napkins and purchase any other items needed for the ceremony and reception. Check with the caterer to see what he/she includes.

_____ Order invitations (25 extra) and personal stationery or "Thank You" notes.

_____ Visit the photographer again to discuss specifics. Use the "Photography Worksheet."

_____ Interview florist, get estimates and order flowers and floral arrangements for wedding and reception. – See our florist interview tool – If you are your own florist, see the flower planning and options tool

_____ Get estimates and order balloons, decorations and favors for wedding and reception.

_____ Book room for wedding night.

_____ Order wedding rings. Allow time for any final engraving.

_____ Order tuxedos for the groomsmen and fathers.

Photographer Interview Questions

Attached are some questions to ask when interviewing photographers, but prior to that, you should think about what you want in terms of wedding photography both in the deliverable, and with the style of photographer and interaction with guests, and the wedding party. Your photographer should be willing to answer these questions and this interview will give you a sense of his or her business temperament. You can ask married friends, or other professionals who run your venue, or cater for you if they have recommendations, but we would still recommend you looking through these questions. Decide which ones are important to you and ask those.

*You should also be prepared to provide the photographer with any needed information such as divorced guests, who do not wish to be photographed together etc.

1. Do you have my date available?

2. Do you have an online portfolio that I, can review to get a sense of your style, and how recent is the material on it?

3. How far in advance do I need to book with you?

4. How long have you been in business/How many weddings have you shot?

5. Are there references you can offer from prior clients or planners? **Note: This is the most important question in the interview.** Do not hire someone who cannot provide you this information, and call at least a couple of the references to compare their answers to your photographer's responses to these questions.

6. How would you describe your photography style (e.g. traditional, photojournalistic, and creative)?

7. How would you describe your approach to interacting with wedding party and guests, i.e. blending in, stirring the pot for creative photos, choreographing shots?

8. What type of equipment do you use?

9. Are you shooting in digital or film format or both?

10. Do you shoot in color and black & white?

11. Can I give you a list of specific shots we would like?

12. How will you (and your assistants) be dressed?

13. Is it okay if other people take photos while you're taking photos?

14. Have you ever shot at (wedding/reception venue)? If not, would you be willing to visit in advance to plan?

15. What time will you arrive at the site and for how long will you shoot?

16. If my event lasts longer than expected, will you stay? Is there an additional charge?

17. Can you put together a slideshow of the bride and groom with provided photos and/or a real time slide show for viewing at the reception?

18. What information do you need from me before the wedding day?

19. What is your rate, and how is ownership of the photos handled? Bride and groom may want to own the photos to copy and use as they see fit, and this may impact price.

20. Are you the photographer who will shoot my wedding? If not, who will shoot it, and can I see their work? If so, who will be assisting you and how?

21. What are your travel charges/requirements if any?

22. Are you photographing other events on the same day as this event?

23. What type of album designs do you offer? Do you provide any assistance in creating an album?

24. Do you provide retouching, color adjustment or other corrective services?

25. How long after the wedding will I get the proofs? Will they be viewable online? On a CD?

26. What is the ordering process?

27. How long after I order my photos/album will I get them?

28. Will you give me the negatives or the digital images, and is there a fee for that?

29. When will I receive a written contract?

30. What is your refund/cancellation policy? Do you have someone who covers your events in case of emergency or equipment failure?

Options for Budget Wedding Photography

1.   Find a local photographer whose style you enjoy, and have the bride and groom take photos in the studio, or at a preferred location. May cost a little, but will be much less expensive than a full day.

2.   Hire a photography student from a local college, by getting references from teachers/professors. Have a backup plan here, and have a contract in place.

3.   Hit up family and friends to see if you have any common connections with talents in photography. Friends and family may want to do this as a wedding gift.

4.   Rather than buying disposable cameras and leaving them on the tables (quality of photos is often not there), ask your guests to bring cameras and set up a photo sharing email address, or drop box. You will love to see what they shoot after the wedding. Sometimes these are the most fun candid moments, you could expect to catch.

5.   Consider using a photography wedding registry. Let guests know, wouldn't you rather that than a toaster anyway?

6.   If your wedding date is off peak, i.e. not Saturday or Sunday, you may be able to get a much better price, since photographers often have much more availability at this time.

7.   Consider using cashback credit points to help pay costs of a photographer who accepts credit cards.

Venue Checklist

This checklist is to be used for interviewing venues, and tracking their answers to insure that they are a good fit for your needs. It is always a good idea to tour the venue early where economics permit, to see for yourself if the place is as nice as the well situated online pictures make it appear to be. When a venue impresses you, be sure to document that, and keep it mind.

Capacity

_____ Reception Area
_____ Theatre/Meeting Room
_____ Dining Area

Caterer

_____ Exclusive caterers?
_____ In-house tables/linens/chairs? If so, check out the quality.
_____ Typical menu cost per head for cocktails, heavy appetizers, etc.
_____ Bar tender charges?
_____ Serving Charges?
_____ Cake cutting charges?
_____ Minimum food and beverage spend?
_____ How early can your caterer arrive day of event to set up?

Rental Fees

_____ Usually negotiable, especially for off days
_____ Does fee include a set up day?
_____ How early/late can you set up take down?

_____   Any discount for payment by check or early payment?

_____   Hotels should waive any room rentals when meet minimum requirements.

Bathrooms

_____   Will you need to provide extra amenities to make the room nicer

_____   Cleanliness – poorly kept restrooms reflect poorly managed venue

_____   Number of stalls vs. number of guests

Parking

_____   Existent?

_____   Fee to use parking lot?

_____   Valets – included? Is there a preferred valet company?

_____   Buses – if using buses - is there room to turn around, unload?

Shipments

_____   Will the venue accept and store boxes a few days before event? Cost?

Audiovisual Team

_____   Exclusive AV Company?

_____   What tech operators are included, if any? (lighting tech, sound, camera)

_____   Cost of in-house AV Team/hour/operator

_____   What AV exists in house? See the quality of the projector and check compatibility.

_____   Internet Access- speed and logistics ($$$)

Stages

_____ Note any restrictions and size dimensions
_____ Height from ground to hang points
_____ See stage lighting with the room dark
_____ Existing backdrops, can you utilize these for event?
_____ If a stage must be brought in understand load-in logistics/restrictions

Registration/Place card area

_____ Is there a clean, open space near entrance of venue and in front of main room?
_____ How much signage can be placed outside of meeting room, in common areas?
_____ Will other events be held during meeting/wedding/party?
_____ Does venue have staff to help with registration/guiding guests to room?

Entrance

_____ Opportunity to brand/decorate entrance area?
_____ Curb appeal; are you comfortable with the current look/feel of the entrance?

Reception Area

_____ How close is the area to the ceremony/meeting room?

_____ Ideally a large open space with the ability to brand/decorate

_____ What furniture can be utilized for event?

_____ Will venue take away existing furniture you don't want for your event?

Any charges?

_____ How early can you set up in this area?

Other Clients

_____ Who else has held events at this venue in recent months?

_____ Testimonials? Can you contact references?

_____ Has a major competitor hosted parties at this venue for a similar client base?

Electronic versions of this tool with room for notes are available upon request at **products@newbizplaybook.com**.

DJ Reception Planning Tool

Agenda:

6:00 PM Guests Arrive.   Background music begins.   Specify
Background Music _____

6:15 PM   Introduction of the Wedding Party. Do you want
                 to have your DJ announce your initial entrance
                 into the reception? If so who,

6:30 PM   Bride/Groom Arrive

6:45 PM   Cocktails: Decide between Classical, Jazz,
                 Traditional New Age, Classic Soft Rock,
                 Contemporary Soft Rock, (Bach, Vivaldi, etc.),
                 (Brubeck, Basie), (Sinatra, Martin, etc.), (Yanni,
                 Enya), (Billy Joel, Elton John, etc.), (Jack Johnson,
                 Jason Mraz, Colbie Caillat, etc.)

7:00 PM   The best man's toast is traditionally done
                 immediately before dinner, but can be done at
                 any time. Please let us know if the father of the
                 bride, the groom, or anyone else wants to say a
                 few short words of welcome.

7:15 PM   Blessing is traditionally done immediately after the
                 toast, and before the dinner is served. If there is a
                 blessing,

7:30   Dinner: Classical, Jazz, Traditional New Age, Classic
                 Soft Rock, Contemporary Soft Rock, (Bach, Vivaldi,
                 etc.), (Brubeck, Basie), (Sinatra, Martin, etc.),
                 (Yanni, Enya), (Billy Joel, Elton John, etc.), (Jack
                 Johnson, Jason Mraz, Colbie Caillat, etc.)

8:15 PM   Traditional Dances. The traditional first dances of the evening will open up the dance floor, after which your guests will be able to dance for the rest of the evening. Typically, you will want to wait until a time when most of your guests are almost through with dinner. Please check off the dances you would like to include, as well as indicating which songs you would like to use for them.

Bride and Groom First Dance Song Title: _____ Artist:_____

Bride/Father Song Title: _____ Artist: _____

Groom/Mother Song Title: _____ Artist: _____

Wedding Party Song Title: _____ Artist:_____

All members of wedding party will dance (parents optional). Some may invite all guests to join ½ way through the song to kick off the dancing. Dance Music Begins.

8:30PM   Cake Cutting. When will you be cutting the cake? Please circle one: As you enter Before Dinner After Dinner

Do you want a special song played at this time? Title:

_____Artist:_____

Would you like us to announce the cake cutting? Yes No

| 9:00PM | Bouquet and Garter Toss. Typically, if a couple chooses to throw the bouquet and/or the garter, they will wait at least 30 minutes after the last Traditional Dance to do so. Background music is usually played while the DJ calls the girls out for the bouquet and if the groom will throw the garter, a fun song is usually played while it is being removed. |

Bouquet Song Title: _____Artist:_____

Garter Song Title:_____ Artist:_____

| 9:30PM | Dollar Dance. As with the bouquet and garter toss, the dollar dance usually happens at least 30 minutes after the last Traditional Dance or immediately after the bouquet and garter toss. The dollar dance is optional. |

DJ Details

What style DJ do you want: Quiet (no interaction during dancing) Moderate (interaction only if necessary) Outgoing (lots of interaction)

Is it more important for you to hear your favorite music, or for your guests to be dancing? _____

How many crowd-involvement songs would you like played (Electric Slide, Duck Dance, Cha Cha Slide, Cupid Shuffle, Anniversary Dance, etc.)?

These questions asked of your client will help to frame the experience they can expect from their DJ.

Catering Interview Questions

1. Do you have references? You want at least two preferably in the last 90 days.

2. Do you have any events that day or weekend? If so, get assurances that both can be accommodated.

3. What services are included in the package, i.e. cooking and delivery only, waiting/food service/bartending, silver and flatware provided?

4. What are your Food/Menu specialties?

5. Pricing and cost options. What courses are included (i.e. appetizer trays, salads, entree's, deserts)?

6. Do you have a liquor license, ability to serve alcohol?

7. What accommodation can you make for dietary needs, allergies, gluten tolerance etc.

8. Are tastings available?

9. Wedding cakes offered?

10. What is the uniform for catering team?

11. Will the catering pro you are interviewing be the one who handles food service?

12. Catering experience handling events the size of your wedding?

13.   Does the caterer have necessary food service licenses?

14.   What are deposit requirements? Be sure to get a full list of charges, including late charges if applicable before paying anything.

Guest List Management Tool

This tool is most easily used in spreadsheet form. An excel file tool is available at newbizplaybook.com. For those who want to download it.

With proper planning, a fair amount of information is needed on each guest including:

1. First and last name

2. Telephone number

3. Address and/or email address

4. Invitation sent

5. Confirmed for attending wedding/or not

6. Confirmed for attending pre-wedding dinner/or not – out of town guests for example

7. Wedding gift

8. Thank you letter sent

Download a great tool for helping the bride and groom keep track of attendance, and their responsibilities for thank you cards etc. This tool also helps the event planner to track and make adjustments for food, dance etc., in the event that more or fewer guests attend than expected. Electronic versions of this spreadsheet will be sent to readers upon request at **products@newbizplaybook.com**.

Important People Contact List

This tool is related, but different. Wedding and event hosts need to have contact information and visibility for VIP guests. If out of town, these folks often won't have cars and other basic amenities at their disposal. This tool allows the people dearest to you to enjoy your event as much as possible. Mistakes made here, create terrible and avoidable regret.

For the VIP guests, you will want to know:

1. Full name

2. Relationship to bride or groom

3. Cell phone if assisting with arrangements

4. Flight information including who will be assisting with transportation (arrivals departures etc.)

5. Hotel details

6. Notes if needed.

We have a spreadsheet tool that will help to track these issues at **products@newbizplaybook.com**.

Florist Interview Questions

1. Do you have my date available?

2. Do you have an online portfolio that I, and/or my client can review to get a sense of your style, and how recent is the material on it?

3. How far in advance do I need to book with you?

4. How long have you been in business/How many weddings have you handled?

5. Are there references you can offer from prior clients or planners? Note: This is the important question in the interview. Do not hire someone who cannot provide you this information, and call at least a couple of the references to compare their answers to your photographer's responses to these questions.

6. Given the size of this wedding, flower preference, color scheme, and venue specifics for church and reception, what would you propose? Note: Do not lead with your budget. Advise that you are open and want to see the proposal for a few different packages, so that you can compare costs.

7. What time will you arrive at the site and how long will it take you to set up?

8. Who will be managing the setup?

9. Are you providing flowers for other events on the same day as this event?

10. Any rental fees for vases or decorations the florist is providing?

11. Any additional labor charges, taxes, or other fee?

12. When will I receive a written contract?

13. What is your refund/cancellation policy? Do you have someone who covers your events in case of emergency? Note: It is common to require a 50% down payment.

Flower Options for Weddings

Wedding

Bride's Flowers

 Bride's bouquet
 Bride's floral crown or hair flowers

Groom Flowers

 Groom's boutonniere
 Groomsmen's' boutonnieres

Wedding Party Flowers

 Bridesmaids' bouquets
 Flower girl's bouquet or basket of pedals
 Ring bearer's boutonniere
 Mother of the bride's corsage
 Mother of the groom's corsage
 Father of the bride's boutonniere
 Father of the groom's boutonniere
 Grandmothers' corsages
 Grandfathers' boutonnieres
 Officiant's boutonniere
 Ushers' boutonnieres

Ceremony Flowers

 Entryway or welcome table arrangements
 Altar/chuppah arrangements
 Pew or chair arrangements
 Candles
 Aisle decorations
 Tossing petals for guests

Reception Flowers

Reception tossing bouquet
Cocktail table arrangements
Bar arrangements
Escort-card table arrangements
Centerpieces
Bride's and groom's chair decorations
Buffet-table/food-station arrangements
Lounge area arrangements
Flowers for wedding cake
Cake table arrangements
Powder room decorations
Getaway car arrangements

Food and Beverage Planning

Appetizers

As you determine the appetizer quantity, consider what purpose the appetizers will serve. If you're serving appetizers before a main meal, you don't need as many as you do if the appetizers are the meal itself. Because appetizers are different from other food items, how much you need depends on several factors. Appetizers don't lend themselves to a quantity chart, per se, but let the following list guide you:

- For appetizers preceding a full meal, you should have at least four different types of appetizers and six to eight pieces (total) per person. For example, say you have 20 guests. In that case, you'd need at least 120 total appetizer pieces.

- For appetizers without a meal, you should have at least six different types of appetizers. You should also have 12 to 15 pieces (total) per person. For example, if you have 20 guests, you need at least 240 total appetizer pieces. This estimate is for a three-hour party. Longer parties require more appetizers.

- The more variety you have, the smaller portion size each type of appetizer will need to have. Therefore, you don't need to make as much of any one particular appetizer.

- When you serve appetizers to a crowd, always include bulk-type appetizers. Bulk-type foods are items that aren't individually made, such as dips or spreads. If you forgo the dips and spreads, you'll end up making hundreds of individual appetizer items, which may push you over the edge. To calculate bulk items, assume 1 ounce equals 1 piece.

- Always try to have extra items, such as black and green olives and nuts, for extra filler.

When appetizers precede the meal, you should serve dinner within an hour. If more than an hour will pass before the meal, then you need to increase the number of appetizers. Once again, always err on the side of having too much rather than too little.

Quantity planning for soups, sides, main courses, and desserts

The following tables can help you determine how much food you need for some typical soups, sides, main courses, and desserts. If the item you're serving isn't listed here, you can probably find an item in the same food group to guide you.

You may notice a bit of a discrepancy between the serving per person and the crowd servings. The per-person serving is based on a plated affair (where someone else has placed the food on the plates and the plates are served to the guests). In contrast, buffet-style affairs typically figure at a lower serving per person because buffets typically feature more side dish items than a plated meal does. Don't use the quantity tables as an exact science; use them to guide you and help you make decisions for your particular crowd. If you're serving a dish that you know everyone loves, then make more than the table suggests. If you have a dish that isn't as popular, you can get by with less.

Soups and Stews

Soup or Stew	Per Person	Crowd of 25	Crowd of 50
Served as a first course	1 cup	5 quarts	2-1/2 gallons
Served as an entree	1-1/2 to 2 cups	2 to 2-1/2 gallons	4 gallons

Main Courses

Entree	Per Person	Crowd of 25	Crowd of 50
Baby-back ribs, pork spareribs, beef short ribs	1 pound	25 pounds	50 pounds
Casserole	N/A	Two or three 9-x-13-inch casseroles	Four or five 9-x-13-inch casseroles
Chicken, turkey, or duck (boneless)	1/2 pound	13 pounds	25 pounds
Chicken or turkey (with bones)	3/4 to 1 pound	19 pounds	38 pounds
Chili, stew, stroganoff, and other chopped meats	5 to 6 ounces	8 pounds	15 pounds
Ground beef	1/2	13 pounds	25 pounds

	pound		
Maine lobster (about 2 lbs. each)	1	25	50
Oysters, clams, and mussels (medium to large)	6 to 10 pieces	100 to 160 pieces	200 to 260 pieces
Pasta	4 to 5 ounces	7 pounds	16 pounds
Pork	14 ounces	22 pounds	44 pounds
Roast (with bone)	14 to 16 ounces	22 to 25 pounds	47 to 50 pounds
Roast cuts (boneless)	1/2 pound	13 pounds	25 pounds
Shrimp (large: 16 to 20 per pound)	5 to 7 shrimp	7 pounds	14 pounds
Steak cuts (T-bone, porterhouse, rib-eye)	16 to 24 ounces	16 to 24 ounces per person	16 to 24 ounces per person
Turkey (whole)	1 pound	25 pounds	50 pounds

Side Dishes

Side Dish	Per Person	Crowd of 25	Crowd of 50
Asparagus, carrots, cauliflower, broccoli, green beans, corn	3 to 4 ounces	4 pounds	8 pounds

kernels, peas, black-eyed peas, and so on

	Per Person	Crowd of 25	Crowd of 50
Corn on the cob (broken in halves when serving buffet-style)	1 ear	20 ears	45 ears
Pasta (cooked)	2 to 3 ounces	3-1/2 pounds	7 pounds
Potatoes and yams	1 (medium)	6 pounds	12 pounds
Rice and grains (cooked)	1-1/2 ounces	2-1/2 pounds	5 pounds

Side Salads

Ingredient	Per Person	Crowd of 25	Crowd of 50
Croutons (medium size)	N/A	2 cups	4 cups
Dressing (served on the side)	N/A	4 cups	8 cups
Fruit salad	N/A	3 quarts	6 quarts
Lettuce (iceberg or romaine)	N/A	4 heads	8 heads
Lettuce (butter or red leaf)	N/A	6 heads	12 heads
Potato or macaroni salad	N/A	8 pounds	16 pounds

Shredded cabbage for coleslaw	N/A	6 to 8 cups (about 1 large head of cabbage)	12 to 16 cups (about 2 large heads of cabbage)
Vegetables (such as tomato and cucumber)	N/A	3 cups	6 cups

Breads

Bread	*Per Person*	*Crowd of 25*	*Crowd of 50*
Croissants or muffins	1-1/2 per person	3-1/2 dozen	7 dozen
Dinner rolls	1-1/2 per person	3-1/2 dozen	7 dozen
French or Italian bread	N/A	Two 18-inch loaves	Four 18-inch loaves

Desserts

Dessert	*Per Person*	*Crowd of 25*	*Crowd of 50*
Brownies or bars	1 to 2 per person	2-1/2 to 3 dozen	5-1/2 to 6 dozen
Cheesecake	2-inch wedge	Two 9-inch cheesecakes	Four 9-inch cheesecakes
Cobbler	1 cup	Two 9-x-9-x-2-inch pans	Four 9-x-9-x-2-inch pans

Cookies	2 to 3	3 to 4 dozen	6 to 8 dozen
Ice cream or sorbet	8 ounces	1 gallon	2 gallons
Layered cake or angel food cake	1 slice	Two 8-inch cakes	Four 8-inch cakes
Pie	3-inch wedge	Two or three 9-inch pies	Four or five 9-inch pies
Pudding, trifles, custards, and the like	1 cup	1 gallon	2 gallons
Sheet cake	2-x-2-inch piece	1/4 sheet cake	1/2 sheet cake

Alcohol and Beverage Planning

Concerning drinks, let the following list guide you:

Soft drinks: One to two 8-ounce servings per person per hour.

Punch: One to two 4-ounce servings per person per hour.

Tea: One to two 8-ounce servings per person per hour.

Coffee: One to two 4-ounce servings per person per hour.

Water: Always provide it. Two standard serving pitchers per table are usually enough.

Again, err on the side of having too much. If people are eating a lot and having fun, they tend to consume more liquid.

Alcohol Consumption and Pricing Projection Tool

There is always some subjectivity in alcohol planning. The assumption here is that 75% of the guests are drinking alcohol. This should be discussed, as a higher percentage of children in attendance, a group of heavier drinkers etc., could impact these assumptions.

As always we recommend adding 10% to all estimates. You will frustrate guests if there is insufficient alcohol, so make sure they are in agreement with your assumptions on numbers. They will know their guests better than anyone. The cost estimates assume average costs on beer, wine, and liquor. Premium beer, wine, and liquor would also mean increased costs. This also assumes equal consumption i.e. 25% each of beer, wine, and liquor. Beer drinkers tend to range closer to 40%, but these figures make scaling for your needs much easier.

The following should help plan for reception alcohol consumption.
BD = beer drinker, WD = wine drinker, LD = liquor drinker

	Small Wedding (100 guests)	
	Amount	Cost
Beer	5 cases per 25 BD	75.00
Wine	20 bottles per 25 WD	160.00
Liquor	6 750 ml bottles per 25 LD	90.00

	Medium Wedding (200 guests)	
	Amount	Cost
Beer	9 cases per 50 BD	135.00
Wine	40 bottles per 50 WD	320.00
Liquor	12 750 ml bottles per 50 LD	180.00

	Large Wedding (100)	
	Amount	Cost
Beer	3 Kegs 100 BD	270.00
Wine	79 bottles per 100 WD	632.00
Liquor	24 750 ml bottles per 100 LD	360.00

Chapter 2 – Inside 60 Days

Much of the tough work is done! Hopefully you have planned through which professionals will help, and have some ideas on firm locations, photography, flowers and food.

If you are your own venue, and/or family friends are hosting the reception at home, or on private land, you have some work to do.

Otherwise, the devil is in the details. Make sure you are checking in regularly to make sure these items are checked off.

_____ Mail invitations (six weeks before the wedding; eight weeks to out-of-town guests).

_____ Finalize arrangements of accommodations for out-of-town attendants and guests.

_____ Buy a wedding gift for future spouse and gifts for attendants and helpers.

_____ Complete the Reception Planner Contact Tool (attached after this chapter) This is hugely important to making sure there are no mistakes or oversites

_____ Decide on Reception Traditions you want to enjoy – see reception planning tool attached after this chapter

_____ If friends or family are acting as DJ, - see order of events planning tool, and dance floor tool after this chapter

_____ If you are renting tables, or linens, see our table and linen planning tools after this chapter to best utilize your space and plan for your guests

Reception Planner Contact Tool

Wedding Details

Wedding Date _____

Wedding Venue Name _____

Rec Venue Name _____

Wedding Venue Address _____

City _____ **Zip** _____

Rec Venue Address _____

City _____ **Zip** _____

Photographer _____

Photographer Phone _____

Videographer _____

Videographer Phone _____

Caterer   _____

Caterer Phone   _____

Electronic versions of this spreadsheet are available upon request at products@newbizplaybook.com.

Wedding Party Contact Tool

Bride & Groom_____   Flower Girl_____

Bride Parents _____   Ring Bearer_____

Groom Parents _____   Minister   _____

Made of Honor _____   Best Man   _____

Gparents Bride _____   Gparents Groom _____

Groom's Men	Brides Maids
1._____	1._____
2._____	2._____
3._____	3._____
4._____	4._____
5._____	5._____
6._____	6._____
7._____	7._____
8._____	8._____

Ushers

1._____   5._____

2._____   6._____

3._____   7._____

4._____   8._____

Traditional Reception Event Planning Tool

Events

Prayer/Grace _____   Toast Best Man _____

Father Bride Toast _____   Father Groom Toast _____

Dad Daughter Dance (song) _____

Mom Groom Dance (song) _____

Bride and Groom 1st Dance _____

Wedding Party (song) _____

Cake   Cutting   (song)   _____

Bouquet Toss (song) _____

Garter (song) _____

Special Requests _____

Groom Comments _____
Bride Comments _____

Special Requests _____

DJ musical genre preference _____

DJ style preference (active vs. camouflage)

Order of Events (please number 1-15)

Introduction	Toast	Father Daughter
Blessing	First Dance	Mother Groom
Bouquet Toss	Last Dance	Cake Cutting
Garter Toss	Other	Other
Other	Other	Other

Dinner Music or Special Songs

1._____ 2._____

3._____ 4._____

5._____ 6._____

7._____ 8._____

9._____ 10._____

11._____ 12._____

Electronic versions of this spreadsheet are available upon request at **products@newbizplaybook.com**.

Dance Floor Planning Tool

This tool has been designed to allow you to plan and scale necessary floor space for dancing. For parties greater than 250, simply use multiples of the tables below. If more than 50% of guests are expected to be dancing, ignore the guests invited column, and plan based upon the number of dancers in the second column.

Total Guests	Dancers	Dance FL Size	Floor SQ Feet
24	12	8'x8'	64
36	18	8'x12'	96
48	24	8'x16'	128
64	32	12'x12'	144
72	36	12'x16'	192
90	45	12'x20	240
96	48	16'x16'	256
120	60	16'x24'	384
128	64	16'x24'	384
144	72	16'x24'	384
150	75	20'x20'	400
168	84	16'x28'	448
180	90	20'x24'	480
192	96	16'x32'	512
210	105	20'x28'	560
250	125	24'x28'	672

Linen Planning Tool

TABLE SIZE	SEATS	54" Sq	80" Sq	90" Sq	72x120"	70x170"	90x132"	90x156"	96" Rnd	108" Rnd	120" Rnd	126" Rnd	132" Rnd
6x30"	4	Overlay	16x29 Drop										
6x30"	6-8			Overlay	26x21 Drop	Box	To Floor All Sides		Overlay, Pinned	Overlay, Pinned	Overlay, Pinned		
6x30"	8-10			Overlay	12x21 Drop	Box		To Floor All Sides	Overlay, Pinned	Overlay, Pinned	Overlay, Pinned		
6x18"	3 (One Side)				24x27 Drop	Box							
6x18"	4 (One Side)				19x27 Drop	Box							
30x30"	4	12" Drop*	29 Drop*	To Floor All Sides									

Linen Planning Tool

TABLE SIZE	SEATS	54" Sq	80" Sq	90" Sq	72x120"	70x170"	90x132"	90x156"	96" Rnd	108" Rnd	120" Rnd	126" Rnd	132" Rnd
30" Round	3	Overlay 12" Drop							To Floor				
3' Round	4	Overlay 9" Drop	Overlay 22" Drop						To Floor				
Café Table	Standing	Overlay 9" Drop	Overlay 22" Drop	Overlay 27" Drop					Overlay 30" Drop		To Floor		
4' Round	6	Overlay Top	Overlay 16" Drop	Overlay 21" Drop					Overlay 24" Drop	To Floor			
5' Round	8–10		Overlay 10" Drop	Overlay 15" Drop					Overlay 18" Drop	Overlay 24" Drop	To Floor		
5.5' Round	9–10		Overlay 7" Drop	Overlay 12" Drop					Overlay 15" Drop	Overlay 21" Drop	27" Drop	To Floor	
6' Round	10–12		Overlay Top	Overlay 9" Drop					Overlay 12" Drop	Overlay 18" Drop	Overlay 24" Drop	27" Drop	To Floor
1/2 Round											1 Cloth, Folded		
Serpentine	Buffet	3 Cloths with 2 Skirts			1 Cloth with 2 Skirts	1 Cloth							

Seating Planning Tool

Banquet Table

Table Size	Seating Capacity	Linen Size	Space Needed
6'	6-8	90" x 132"	11" x 7"
8'	8-10	90" x 156"	13' x 7'
Classroom 6'	4	70" x 170"	11' x 6'
Classroom 8'	6	70" x 170"	13' x 6'

Round Table

Table Size	Seating Capacity	Linen Size	Space Needed
2.5'	2-4	96" round	7' diameter
3'	4-5	96" round	8' diameter
4'	6-8	108" round	9' diameter
5'	8-10	120" round	10' diameter
6'	10-12	132" round	11' diameter

Cocktail Table

Table Size	Seating Capacity	Linen Size	Space Needed
2.5'	2-4	108" round	7' diameter
3'	4-5	120" round	8' diameter

Chapter 3 - 30 Days or More Before

If Chapter 2 was about details, this chapter is even more finely focused on those same details. This is for the most part about beauty and courtesy.

Be sure to look at the packing tool and week of wedding tool, to make sure everyone understands their responsibilities.

We have some tools to help make sure there are no mistakes!

_____ Ready all accessories, shoes and lingerie for bridal gown – we have attached a great packing tool checklist at the end of this chapter

_____ Obtain gifts for bridesmaids, and groomsmen

_____ Have beauty consultant do a trial run with bride's hair and makeup. Schedule this appointment on the day the bridal portrait is taken and/or a party is planned or schedule on the day of your final dress fitting to see exactly how you will look on wedding day. If a friend or family member is helping here, give them a trial run!

_____ Have final fitting for bridal gown and bridesmaids' dresses.

_____ Have bridal portrait taken. If you are on a tight photography budget, consider in studio, or remote photos of traditional wedding poses with bride and groom at lower expense.

_____ Have groomsmen registered and measured at the formal wear store. Groom should rent a tux if taking photos with bride

_____ Check with the newspapers on wedding announcement requirements.

_____ Finalize plans for rehearsal dinner. Make sure plans for toasts etc., are clear to those who will be expected to offer them

_____ Plan seating arrangements for the rehearsal dinner and reception.

_____ Review this checklist to be sure nothing has been missed.

_____ Complete change-of-address information for post-office.

_____ Keep current with "Thank You" notes for shower and early wedding gifts.

Two weeks before:

_____ Get the marriage license. Be sure to bring all needed documents.

_____ Inform or send rehearsal invitations including exact time and location to those who will attend the rehearsal and rehearsal dinner.

_____ Inquire about where bride, groom and attendants will dress for the ceremony.

_____ Review all details. Walk through the entire event considering things like parking, access for handicapped guests, etc.

_____ Confirm all transportation plans.

_____ Check in with caterer, photographer, videographer, musicians, DJ, florist, etc. or those helping with these items to confirm all arrangements.

_____ "Break in" wedding shoes at home

One week before:

_____ Appoint someone to act as an "organizer" to handle any last minute problems.

_____ Give a final guest count to the caterer, or make adjustments to food budgeting and planning .

_____ Review final details for those in the wedding party.

_____ Confirm honeymoon arrangements.

_____ Pack for the honeymoon.

_____ Enjoy a day with family and friends. Visit a day spa, have a massage, a facial and relax.

One day before:

_____ Attend the rehearsal and rehearsal dinner and give gifts to attendants.

_____ Give the rings and clergy's fee to the best man.

_____ Organize gown, accessories, etc. to go to ceremony.

_____ Get a manicure and pedicure.

On the wedding day:

_____   Mail wedding announcements.

_____   Get hair, makeup, etc. done.

_____   Enjoy the day!

Electronic versions of this tool with room for notes are available upon request at **products@newbizplaybook.com**

Packing Planning Tool

As silly as it sounds, one of the most common "emergencies," that plague weddings and events is forgotten items, missing clothing, or lost guest books etc. We have a spreadsheet tool to track these issues at **products@newbizplaybook.com**.

General Items	Box Number	Location for Wedding	Goes home with...
Pre-Ceremony Bride			
Dress/Suit	freestanding	Hotel Room	Sara Smith
Headpeice	freestanding	Hotel Room	Sara Smith
Jewelry	freestanding	Hotel Room	Mrs. Bride's Mom
Ring	freestanding	Hotel Room	Bride
Shoes	freestanding	Hotel Room	Sara Smith
Suitcase	freestanding	Hotel Room	Sara Smith
Wedding Party Gifts	1	Parents House	Mrs. Groom's Mom
Pre-Ceremony Groom			
Tux	freestanding	Hotel Room	Joe Jones
Jewelry	freestanding	Hotel Room	Groom
Shoes	freestanding	Hotel Room	Joe Jones
Tie, cuff links, etc	freestanding	Hotel Room	Joe Jones
Ring	freestanding	Hotel Room	Groom
Suitcase	freestanding	Hotel Room	Mrs. Groom's Mom
Wedding Party Gifts	3	Parents House	Mrs. Groom's Mom
Ceremony			
Flowers	freestanding	B Parents House	Given to guests
Decorations	4	B Parents House	Given to guests
Wedding signs	freestanding	Parents House	Mrs. Bride's Mom
Pre-Reception Bride			
Rec Dress	freestanding	Hotel Room	Sara Smith
Jewelry	freestanding	Hotel Room	Bride
Shoes	freestanding	Hotel Room	Sara Smith
Reception			
Cake Cutter for guests	1	Parents House	Planner
Glue, Scissors, Pens,	1	Parents House	Planner
Escort Cards	2	B Parents House	Planner
Escort Card Board	freestanding	G Parents House	Planner
Guest book,	2	gParents House	Planner
Garters	2	Parents House	Planner
Cake Knife For Pictures	2	Parents House	Planner
Kids Table Kits	2	Parents House	Planner
Etc.			
CPR Paddles		1 Church/Venue	
Parking Lot Signs	freestanding	Venue	Planner
Sewing Kit	1	Church/Venue	Planner
Deodorant/ etc	1	Church/Venue	Planner
Hair pins/ supply	1	Church/Venue	Planner
Emergency Kit	1	Church/Venue	Planner
Step stool	freestanding	Church/Venue	Planner

Week of Wedding Schedule Tool

Time	Event	Location	Responsible Organizer
3:30 PM	Bride and Bridesmaids Arrive,	Bride's Apt	Maiden of Honor
4:30 PM	Rehearsal	The Church	Couple, Wedding Party
5:00 PM	Set up for Rehearsal Dinner	Groom's Parents' House	Groom, Groom's Parents
5:00 PM	Caterer arrives; begins set-up	Groom's Parents' House	Caterer
5:30PM	Couple arrives	Groom's Parents' House	The Couple
6:00 PM	Guests arrive	Groom's Parents' House	Everyone
7:00 PM	Food served	Groom's Parents' House	Caterer
8:15 PM	Caterer packs up	Groom's Parents' House	Caterer
9:30 PM	Couple leaves	Groom's Parents' House	The Couple
10:00 PM	Clean-up	Groom's Parents' House	Groom's Parents & volunteers
Begin at 7:30 AM	*SEE DAY OF SPREADSHEET*		
10:00 AM	Post Wedding Brunch	Acme Restaurant	Best Man and Maiden of Honor

Proper organization insures that everyone knows where to be and when. In many instances, there may be a need to add or remove events, change times, locations, or even responsible organizer. This tool allows everyone to be on the same page. The responsible organizer examples above are not intended to be a comment as to who should traditionally handle what. They are only present as an example. Electronic versions of this spreadsheet are available upon request at **products@newbizplaybook.com**.

Day of Wedding Schedule Tool

When	What	Where	Who
	Pre-Ceremony		
7:00 AM	Bride wakes up	Bride's Apt	Bride
7:30 AM	Friends arrive to do hair & makeup	Bride's Apt	Bride + friends
8:00 AM	pick up decorations	Wedding Planner Storage	Wedding Stage Manager
8:15 AM	Photographer arrives	Church	Photographer
8:30 AM	Church opens	Church	Wedding Stage Manager
8:30 AM	set up begins	Church	wedding party
8:15 AM	Bride and Groom Leave for Church	Church	Couple
8:45 AM	Photographer leaves for venue	Church	Photographer
8:45 AM	sound system check	Church	Wedding Singer
9:00 AM	Photographer arrives for photos	Church	Photographer + Couple
9:15 AM	Family Arrives for photos	Church	Wedding Party & Family
9:30 AM	Family Photos	Church	Photographer + Family + Couple
9:30 AM	flowers set up at Chruch	Church	Florist
9:50 AM	Wedding party photos	Church	Couple
10:30 AM	Reception set up begins	Venue	wedding party
11:30 AM	Final Wedding Touch ups Minister Arrives	Church	Minister and wedding party family
11:45 AM	Usher's take their places and begin seating	Church	ushers
12:15 PM	Guests are all seated and Wedding Party in Place	Church	all
12:20 PM	Wedding Ceremony	Church	all
1:00 PM	Couple + Wedding Party get ready	Getting Ready Area	Couple + Wedding Party

Day of Wedding Schedule Tool

Time	Event	Location	Who
Cocktail Hour			
1:30 PM	Couple Quiet time	take a walk	couple
1:55 PM	cocktail hour	venue	Wedding Stage Manager/ caterer
2:00 PM	Couple Photos	venue	photog., couple
2:15 PM	Couple joins party	venue	couple
Reception			
10:00 AM	cake picked up from bakery	bakery address	Reception Manager
2:30 PM	guest seated for brunch	venue	Wedding Stage Manager/ caterer
3:00 PM	toasts - four total	dance floor	names of toast givers
4:15 PM	meal over	venue	Wedding Stage Manager/ caterer
5:00 PM	first dance	dance floor	couple
5:35 PM	dance Bride and Dad Groom and Mom	dance floor	all
6:00 PM	cake cutting	venue	Wedding Stage Manager cues
6:05 PM	dance	dance floor	all
11:30 PM	last call	venue	announced by Wedding Stage Manager
11:45 PM	Send off	venue	Wedding Stage Manager cues
12:00 PM	guests out	venue	Wedding Stage Manager cues
Post-Reception			
5:00 PM	caterer & family start breakdown	venue	caterer/ family
10-12:30 PM	families leave with stuff they're taking	venue	family
1:00 AM	breakdown done, everyone out	venue	all

These are only present as an example. Electronic versions of this spreadsheet are available upon request at **products@newbizplaybook.com**

Extra Tools to Help For the Big Day

Most of these are available in electronic form at **products@newbizplaybook.com**.

Wedding Budget Tool

In the attachments, we have included an excel spreadsheet complete with all formulas and entries needed for a great wedding budget tool. You can add items, or leave 0's in emails that don't apply. This tool will help you and your clients plan costs, and adjust in real time for increased costs or savings to allow the necessary flexibility.

The below is a print version you can complete as needed, electronic spreadsheet available at products@newbizplaybook.com

Total Budgeted Amount	
Guest Headcount (you can change this to see the figures below adjust)	
Ceremony	
Gown & Alterations	
Veil & Headpiece	
Bride's Accessories (lingerie, shoes, gloves, etc.)	
Bride's Hair & Makeup	
Bridesmaids Hair	
Bridesmaids wraps & purses	
Groomens Ties	
Site Fee	
Ceremony AV	
Officiant's Fee	
License and copies (4 @ $15 each)	
Accessories (arch, runner, etc.)	
Hotel	
Valet or Parking	
Food & Services ($X/Guest)	
Beverages & Bartenders ($40.00/Guest)	
Wedding Cake	
Recpetion Set up fees/dance floor	
Tax & Tip on food	
Florals	
Bridal Bouquet	
Flowers For Bride's Attendants ($60/Bride Attendant)	
Flowers For Groom's Attendants ($25/Groom Attendant)	
Other florals for guests	
tax on flowers	

Reception Centerpieces & Decor ($80 each*12)	
Children	
Child Care	
TV Rental	
Children's Meals	
Entertainment	
Ceremony Musician	
Reception Band	
Photographer	
Videographer	
Guests	
Shuttle Rental ($150/first run, $100 additional)	
Bride & Groom's Hotel Rooms	
Attendant Gifts ($x/Attendant)	
Donation/Favors ($x/Guest)	
Welcome Baskets ($x ea.)	

Printed Materials	
Invitations (reply cards, calligraphy, postage, etc.)	
Other Stationery (programs, thank you notes)	
Menu cards	
Welcome Party Invites/Rehearsal Dinner Invites	
TOTAL:	

Festivities around Wedding:	
(often these are covered by a parent or a separate budget)	
Bridesmaids Brunch	
	Tax/Tip 28%
Groomsmen Golf Outing	
Food on course	
Welcome Party	
food	
Alcohol	

	Tax
Rehearsal Dinner	
food	
alcohol	
Reception hall rental	
equipment rental (margarita machines lights etc.)	
silverware rental/ linen costs/plate & crystal costs	
waitstaff/bartenders	
decorations	
fun photo booth etc.	
Tip/Tax	Tax/Tip 28%
Total Wedding Festivities:	

Electronic versions of this spreadsheet are available upon request at **products@newbizplaybook.com**.

Vendor Contact Planning Sheet

Vendor	Business Name	Contact Name	Contact Number	Payment Status
Photographer				
Minister/Rabi				
Bakery				
Bar Tenders				
Wait staff				
Caterer				
Videographer				
D.J.				
Flowers				

Vendor Commitment Sheet

Vendor	Commitment	Arrival Time	Notes -	Gets Meal -
Photographer	8 hours x2			
Minister/Rabi				
Bakery		2.pm		
Bar Tenders				
Wait staff				No
Caterer				
Videographer				
D.J.				
Flowers				

Other Wedding Budget Saving Tips

1. **Linens:** House linens are free at hotels and restaurants and often perfectly acceptable.

2. **Dates:** Move your wedding to the Summer and book a Thursday or Friday night event, venue, and professional caterer, photographer, florist, DJ pricing will be much less expensive.

3. **Restaurants:** Restaurants rarely charge rental fees for private rooms, however hotels or special event venues usually do.

4. **Engagement length:** Longer engagements if possible, allow for earlier booking, which can lock in lower costs.

5. **Valets:** Booking a venue that already has valet service will save several hundred dollars an hour for a large event.

6. **Centerpieces:** Candles or an exquisite dessert tower is usually far less than flowers.

7. **Venue:** Select venues that do not require you to use their services.

8. **Alcohol:** If your group enjoys their vino, work out a cost/head rather than volume with your venue or caterer.

9.   **School:** Consider having your event on campus, which often have great facilities at discounts for students and alumni.

10. **Decor:** Lighting can be a great way to set a mood and using colored gels on a blank wall can have a major impact for little money.

11. **Hotel Rooms:** Hotels often provide you with a "staff room" rate – get as many of these rooms as you can for your team.

12. **Food:** Consider not having a sit down dinner, with appetizers and finger foods set out for guests to snack on.

13. **Sharing a Venue:** Anytime you can book a venue with another group for back to back nights you can save on major ticket items like the AV, chair rentals, decor, stage sets, etc.

14. **Fake Cakes:** Most bakers have cardboard cutouts that can be used for tiers. Set the top as a real cake to be cut by bride and groom for photos. Serve guests sheet cakes from the kitchen.

15. **Alcohol:** Offer a couple of kegs, and a signature drink to keep costs low.

16. **Flowers:** Consider supplying your own by purchasing flowers from wholesale florists.

17. **Photobooth:** Build your own. There are tons of plans for PVC booths that can be built for less than 50$.

18. **Wedding Dress:** Rent it! You can find inexpensive rentals that are vastly less expensive than purchasing one forever.

19. **Stationary:** Stuff the envelopes yourself! It is much cheaper than paying a stationer 7$ per.

20. **Jewelry:** Rent the ice! Beautiful costume jewelry is also available very inexpensively.

Do Your Own Piping Draping Tool

Installation Instructions for Pipe & Drape

Equipment Included:

- **Base Plates**
- **Aluminium Uprights**
- **Adjustable Sliders**
- **Panels of Drape**

Instructions for Set-Up

I. Adjust Aluminum Drape Support _____ to the desired length and lock into place. Lay the sliders on the floor in the area in which you will up the drape.

Note: Sliders will adjust between 7' and 12'.

II. Place base plates down on each side of the adjustable sliders and insert aluminum uprights onto base plates as shown on diagram below.

Note: Ensure that the slots on the aluminum uprights are at the top and not at the bottom, as this is where the adjustable sliders will hook into.

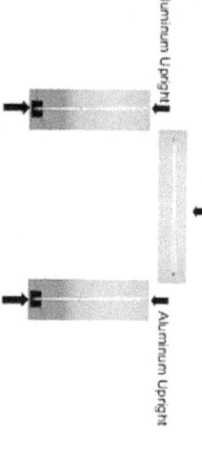

Aluminium Upright

Base Plate

Adjustable Slider

Aluminium Upright

Base Plate

III. Thread drape panels (seam side back) onto slider and hook slider onto aluminum. If you find that the aluminums are too high, hook only one side of slider holding it at a 45 degree angle when threading drape onto adjustable slider. Prior to installation, drape panels are 3' wide. Upon installation of the drape, please gather each drape panel to reflect a width of 2' of draping which gives the finished product a richer look as it appears fuller from the gathers.

Instructions for Dismantling:

To remove drape, unhook one side of the adjustable slider from the aluminum upright, drop slider to a 45 degree angle to permit the drape to slide off of them. Detach slider from remaining side. Fold up drape panels and place into tubs provided, and adjust sliders back to their original position. Place all aluminum uprights, sliders and base plates back in the storage boxes provided.

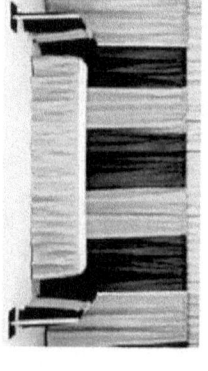

Tent Rental Guidelines

If you are planning an event outdoors, where cooperation of rain is at issue, you must consider the potential for a need for tents.

1.   Hearing toasts or music in a tent can be difficult. You will need microphones and av help if you are in one.

2.   Temperature can be hard to control in a tent. Best to use a tent in moderate environments, rather than Atlanta in July.

3.   You can rent heat or air conditioning units, but listen to them first. Some are extraordinary loud.

4.   Food Prep areas should be planned for as well if needed for the catering teams. This area can be a separate tent or simply a small 10x10 walled in area near the main tent.

5.   Power. Will you need generators? Don't assume that the home, or venue that you are using has sufficient power to cover all needs for lighting etc. inside the tent.

6.   Tents take a while to set up. Insist it be done the day before. Trust us on this.

7.   Make sure you are using a v-line roof tent, preferably with clear windows on the sides. This provides height for comfort, and allows for keeping out rain and temps without claustrophobia.

8.   Tent needs to be staked or held down by water barrels. No corner cutting for these. We have seen tents take flight like kites. People can be hurt or worse.

9.   Tents are heavy. Consider how transportation will be able to get to the spot where you want the tent.

10.   Ask your tent company to draw out how the guest tables and any buffet tables will be set up. You want to be sure there is enough room for guests, caterers, and servers, to walk comfortably between tables.

NOTES:

NOTES: